# Starting from Scratch

## A Kid's Guide to Learning to Code

Rumaysa and Zayd Ahmed

ISBN: 9798872230601 (paperback)

# CONTENTS

# ABOUT THE BOOK

Welcome to 'Starting From Scratch'! We're JUSTCodaborate, an online community of creative young coders and programmers from all over the world. We've made this book because we want all young people to be able to develop games. We would like to teach you that coding is fun, alongside creating some exciting projects. Coding is one of the most important things you can learn and now is the perfect time to do it in our ever growing technological world.

## Who is this book for?

This book is for anyone interested in learning to code, however old you are, wherever you come from, whatever you know about coding already – this book is for everyone! You can start from whichever point you'd like, or if you know about Scratch already, you can create just the projects!

## What will this book teach you?

Computers can do absolutely anything, but first, somebody (like you!) needs to write a program/code for it to follow. Computer programs have to be written in languages computers understand. For example, we speak in languages like English, Arabic, Spanish, Swedish, German and many more, but computers don't. Coding involves giving instructions to computers to perform certain actions and logical thinking.

This book will show you how you can use Scratch, a block-based programming language, for all sorts of wonderful creations.

## What do I need?

You have two choices – you can code offline on your computer/laptop or code online. Find out how on page 6. And besides this, you also need a willingness to learn, an imagination, some confidence and creativity!

# MEET THE CHARACTERS

Meet Isaac, Zahra, Caleb and Tenshi – four friends who *love* Scratch! They will appear every now and then throughout the book, sometimes giving tips, other times making jokes or just being a little source of motivation!

Isaac          Zahra          Caleb          Tenshi

# SETUP

To complete the projects in this book, you can choose to either code using the online Scratch editor or offline on your computer. Always get a grown-up's permission before installing or downloading anything on your device.

You can watch this video on how to download Scratch to Windows 10 or 11: https://youtu.be/69kcaEOybjE

As well as being downloaded to Windows, Scratch can also be used on MacOS, a Chromebook or an Android tablet.

If you'd like to use the online version of Scratch, you will need to be connected to the Internet.

## Online

1. Open your web browser.
2. Go to https://scratch.mit.edu/join.
3. Create a username.
4. Create a password and click 'Next'.
5. Select your country (optional) and click 'Next'.
6. Enter your month and year of birth then click 'Next'.
7. Select a gender from the list and click 'Next'.
8. Enter an email address then click 'Create Your Account'.
9. Check your email to verify your account.

## Offline (any device)

1. Open your web browser.
2. Go to https://scratch.mit.edu/download.
3. Select your operating system (OS) from one of the options (Windows, MacOS, Chromebook or Android).
4. If Windows or MacOS is selected: click the native app store links or 'Direct Download'.
5. If ChromeOS or Android is selected: click 'Get it on Google Play'.
6. Follow the instructions to download Scratch on your device.

# THE SCRATCH INTERFACE

This is the online Scratch interface.

The offline version is similar!

In this section, you will be introduced to the Scratch interface before you begin making projects. This is important because you will need to know where to find things!

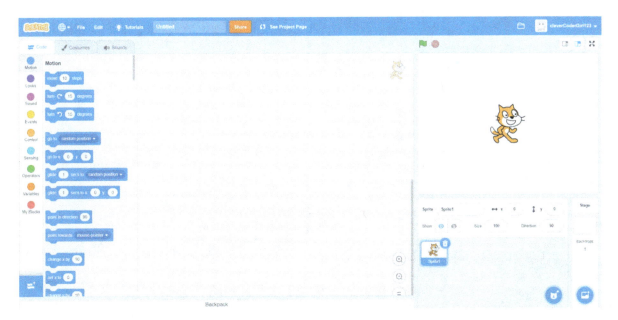

On the right-side is the **stage**. The far left shows the code palette and the middle is the code area. Let's look at each section in a little more detail.

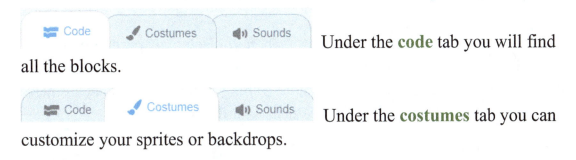

Under the **code** tab you will find all the blocks.

Under the **costumes** tab you can customize your sprites or backdrops.

7

Under the **sounds** tab you can add sounds to your projects.

**Backdrops** are the backgrounds for your **stage**. You can create your own, get ones from the library or upload a backdrop from your device.

The **sprites** are the characters or objects in your project.

This is the default cat **sprite** added to all new projects in the Scratch editor.

When you select a **sprite**, you can change its name, its position on the **x** and **y** axes, make it bigger or smaller, rotate it or choose whether or not to show or hide it. You can also customize all of this using code. Let's take a closer look at that.

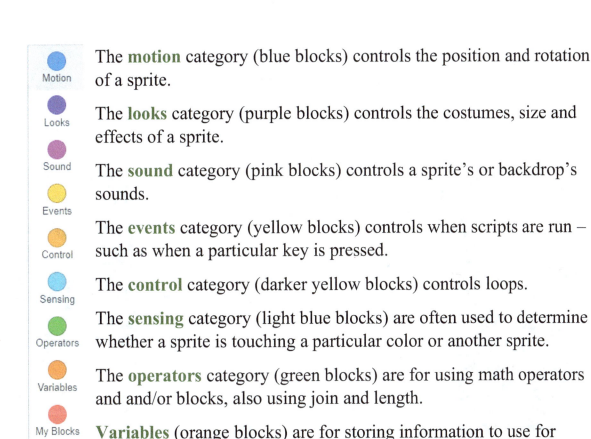

The **motion** category (blue blocks) controls the position and rotation of a sprite.

The **looks** category (purple blocks) controls the costumes, size and effects of a sprite.

The **sound** category (pink blocks) controls a sprite's or backdrop's sounds.

The **events** category (yellow blocks) controls when scripts are run – such as when a particular key is pressed.

The **control** category (darker yellow blocks) controls loops.

The **sensing** category (light blue blocks) are often used to determine whether a sprite is touching a particular color or another sprite.

The **operators** category (green blocks) are for using math operators and and/or blocks, also using join and length.

**Variables** (orange blocks) are for storing information to use for later – such as a score.

The red blocks are for creating custom blocks. We don't look at those in this book.

This is the green flag and the red stop button. The green flag is for running projects (an **events** block can detect if it's pressed) and the red stop button cancels all scripts running.

Backpack

Loading...

If you use the online Scratch editor, the above image is your backpack. You can store scripts, costumes, backdrops and sprites here to use in other projects.

Under the **costumes** tab, you can customize the look of your sprites. You can use code to control which costumes to switch to and when.

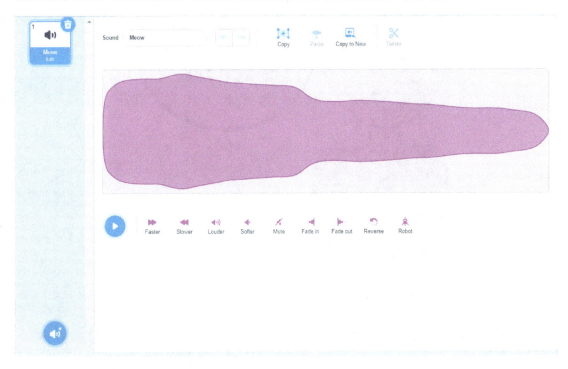

Under the **sounds** tab, you can use sounds from the library or record your own. In this chapter, there will be a section that discusses what you can do in the Scratch sound editor.

## Creating Your First Script

The first thing we're going to do is create a basic script.

Make sure the cat sprite is selected as shown below. Go to the **code** tab.

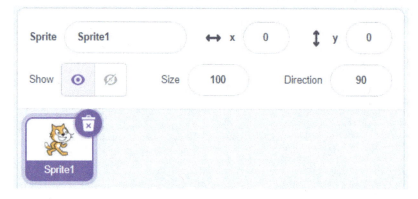

From **events**, add a **when green flag clicked** block. Go to the **Motions** tab and add a **move 10 steps** block. You should have this in your code area:

12

Click the green flag and the cat should move!

Let's change things up a bit! Delete the move block. Go to the **Control** section and add a **forever** block. The **forever** block will run whatever blocks are inside it over and over until the script is stopped (e.g. pressing the red stop button). In the **forever** block, add one of the **turn 15 degrees** blocks and click the green flag. The cat should now be endlessly rotating!

To slow it down, let's add a **wait** block from **Control**. If one second is too fast or too slow, decrease or increase the number. Here's an example:

Two tenths of a second isn't too slow or too fast either!

Next, we'll try adding a **go to random position** block. Add it after the **turn** block. The cat always rotates a little bit before going to a different place. Now change the wait time and put the **turn** block before it. The cat now turns, waits and moves elsewhere.

In Scratch, code always runs in the order you put it. If you wanted the cat to start in the center of the stage, you can add a **go to x 0 y 0** block before the **forever** block. If you want it to start pointing the right way, you can add a **point in direction 90** block. Here's an example:

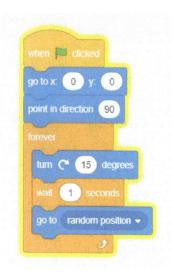

Click the green flag and see the difference for yourself!

## Switching the Costumes and Backdrops

Next, we're going to look at switching costumes and backdrops with code.

First, delete the cat **sprite** by clicking the bin button. Next, click on this button:

 Pick a different sprite. Change its **x** and **y** axes to 0.

Add a backdrop.

Making sure your new sprite is selected, add a **when green flag clicked** block. Add a **wait** block. After that, go to the **Looks** section and add the **next costume** block.

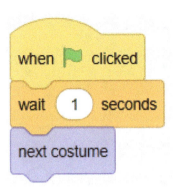

Click the green flag and you should see the sprite switch costumes!

Now that we have two backdrops (the white one and a new one), we can also add code to the backdrops (or your new sprite) to change the background of the stage. Click the **Stage** tab and add a **when green flag clicked** block. Now go to **Looks** and add a **switch backdrop to backdrop1**. Add a **wait** block and a **switch backdrop** to your new one. You should see the stage start with the white background and then change to your new one! Here's an example of the code:

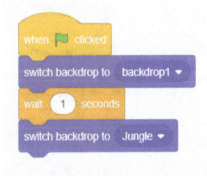

Try it out!

## The Repeat Block

The **repeat** block is very similar to the **forever** block. It can run a script for a specific number of times. However, unlike the **forever** block, you can run other scripts once the loop is over. Here's an example:

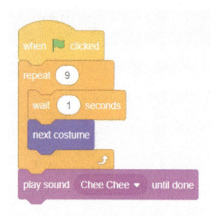

Try something similar too!

## Sounds in Scratch

As well as a sprites, costumes and backdrops library, Scratch also has a sounds library. With Scratch's great tools, you can customize and edit sounds.

By dragging your mouse over the sound visualization, you can copy, paste and delete different parts of a sound, as well as using the buttons above.

This is what you see below the visualization:

You can change the speed of the sound, change the volume, reverse the sound or make it sound a little like a robot. Those are some of the great things Scratch's sound editor can do!

## Code Exercise!

To try out some of the skills you've learned, you're going to make a running animation! It will use a few blocks of code with some concepts covered already.

For this, we have already provided the backdrops you'll need. Follow the instructions below depending on the environment you have chosen to use.

## Online

1. Make sure you're signed into your Scratch account. Go to the following link: https://scratch.mit.edu/projects/727476837
2. Click the turquoise **Remix** button. You now have the backdrops for this project.

## Offline

1. Open your browser.
2. Go to the following link: https://scratch.mit.edu/projects/727476837
3. Click the blue  button.
4. Click **File** and select **Save to Your Computer**.
5. Open the Scratch app.
6. Click **File** and **Load From Your Computer**.
7. Open the file you just downloaded. You now have the backdrops for this project.

Make sure the stage is selected.

Go through each backdrop. We're going to start the animation from **backdrop12**.

To start with, we need a **when green flag clicked** block. Since we're starting from **backdrop12**, we need a **switch backdrop to backdrop12** block as well.

For this animation, we'll endlessly loop through the backdrops. We can do this with a **forever** block.

What do you think should go in the **forever** block?

If we add a **next backdrop** block and click the green flag, what do you notice? Is the animation too fast or too slow?

What do you think we can add to the **forever** block to speed it up or slow it down?

This is an example:

Give it a go and see what it gives you! You can adjust the speed as you wish.

## Extensions

At the bottom of the screen, you might see an icon like this:

 This button is for adding extension blocks. You will see something like this:

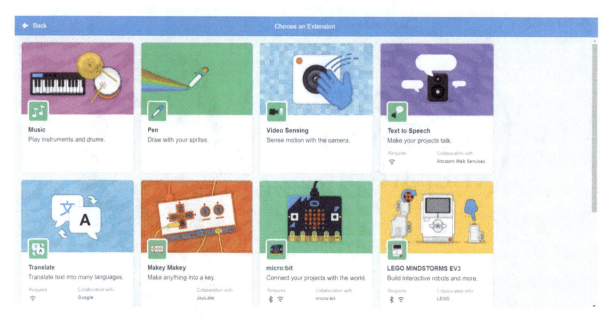

In this section, we will discuss using the Music, Text to Speech and Translate extensions. If you're interested in learning how to use the other extensions, there are many fantastic tutorials on the Internet that can show you how.

## Conditionals

In programming, a conditional is checking if a condition is true or not. In Scratch, we can do this with an **if** block, **if-else** block or a **repeat until**

block. These are very useful when you want to check if two things are different or are the same. This is what Scratch's conditional blocks look like:

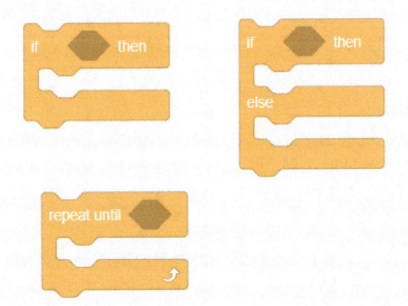

These blocks are often used with blocks in the **Sensing** and **Operators** categories, as well as occasionally with **variables**.

Conditionals usually return something called a **boolean**, which is either **true** or **false**.

## Sensing and the Say Block

As mentioned before, **sensing** blocks are usually used to detect things in your project – such as when a key is pressed or a sprite touches a color or another sprite. However, there are two sensing blocks which you can use and attach to most other blocks.

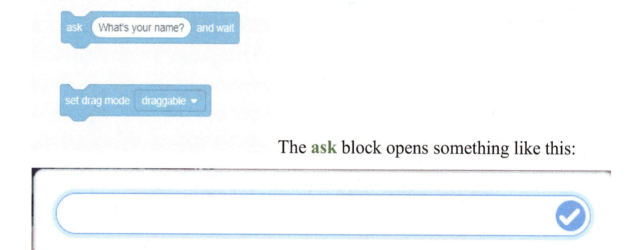

The **ask** block opens something like this:

The **set drag mode** block has two values – draggable and not draggable. This is if you want to enable dragging a sprite in full screen or disable dragging sprites in full screen.

This is to find out what was entered in the answer box.

We can use the say block to return what was entered by the user with the following code:

And it can return this:

Try it out for yourself!

## Operators Blocks

The **Operators** blocks can be used for calculations and comparisons. It can also be used to join text together, pick random numbers, get the length of a word and much more to explore and discover.

We're now going to experiment with some of the **Operators** blocks to practice the use of **Conditionals**.

First of all, return to the project we were in before we made the running animation. Make sure your sprite is selected. Delete the **repeat** block code from earlier. In your code area, you should now have a **when green flag clicked** block only. Go to the **Control** section and add an **if-else** block. Go to **Operators** and add a **greater than** block. Enter any number in the empty box before the > sign. In the **if** section, add a **say** block which can say something like 'the number is greater than fifty'. In the **else** section, add a **say** block with something like 'the number is less than fifty'. Here are two examples:

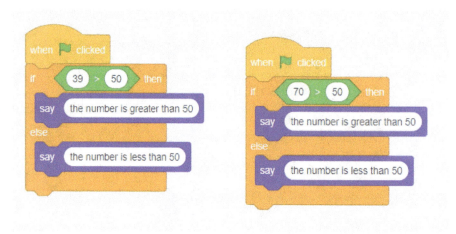

They both return:

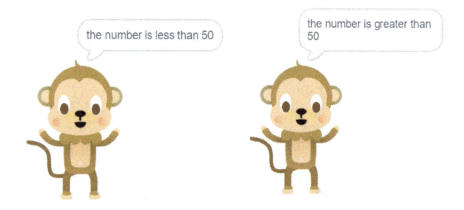

As you can see, the first conditional checked if thirty-nine was greater than fifty. That's false, so it returned the **say** block in the **else** section. In the second conditional, seventy was greater than fifty, so it returned the **say** block from the first section.

## Broadcasts

**Broadcast** blocks are helpful blocks which are used for sending 'messages' to other sprites, scripts or maybe even the backdrop!

When the message is received, it will perform a specific action because of that message. The **broadcast** blocks are great for making games!

Here's an example:

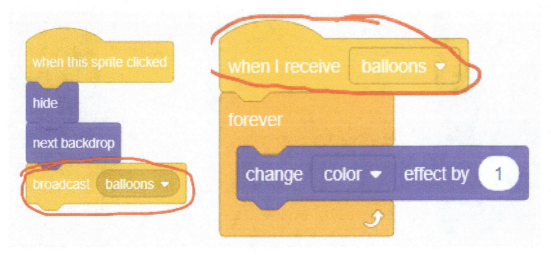

In the first script, we **broadcast** a message for when a sprite is clicked. In the second script, we use a **forever** block and a **change colour effect** block when the message (called **balloons**) is received.

## Variables

Variables are arguably one of the most useful Scratch blocks. They can be used for counting clicks in a clicker game, counting goals in a football match, being used as a countdown or even storing something that you answered before.

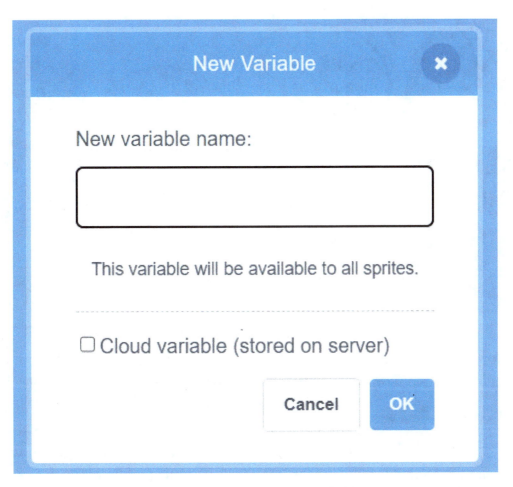

The **set variable** block can set the value of a variable. You can only store one thing in a variable.

To store different types of data, you will need to create several different ones – or a list, but we won't cover that in this book. You also have the option to  show the variable on the screen, or you can hide it. If you right click on the variable when it is showing on-screen, you have the option to change the way it is displayed. In fact, you can even change it to a slider, where people can change the value of the variable without going into the script.

Variables, as we said before, are very useful. Sliders may not come in for the projects we are going to make, but you can do as much experimenting with them as you would like.

Now that you have an idea how the Scratch interface works, it's time to get started with making projects!

# PROJECT 1 – VIRTUAL CARD

Welcome to your first project – a virtual card! You can use this for any occasion…a birthday, a celebration or maybe even an achievement! This will use **looks**, **sounds** and **events** blocks as well as **control** ones too!

For this project, we will have six sprites – a button to open the card, four balloons that will pop and text with a message. We will also add some sound effects and music and use a backdrop from the Scratch library.

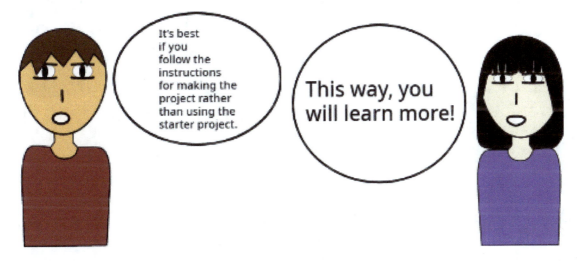

However, we will still provide all the necessary sprites, sounds and backdrops. Follow the instructions depending on which editor you are using.

## Online

1. Make sure you're signed into your Scratch account. Go to the following link: https://scratch.mit.edu/projects/844340121
2. Click the turquoise **Remix** button. You now have the basic sprites and backdrops for this project.

## Offline

1. Open your browser.

2. Go to the following link: https://scratch.mit.edu/projects/844340121
3. Click the blue **See inside** button.
4. Click **File** and select Save to Your Computer. In the second step of the project, you will be able to load the starter material in the Scratch app.

## Step 1: Create a new project

To start this project, you will need to open Scratch. You can either sign into your Scratch account online or open the app on your device.

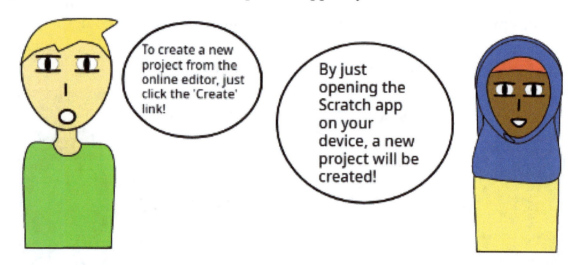

## Step 2: Load the starter project (offline only)

Once the Scratch editor is open, click **File** and select **Load from Your Computer**. Open the starter project from your file explorer.

## Step 3: Adding a backdrop and sound

First of all, delete the cat sprite.

Next, we will add the party background.

Keep the white background, as well still need it before the card is opened.

When the card is opened, we will also want to play sound to make it more interesting. Under the **sounds** tab, click the choose a sound button (in the bottom left corner) to select a sound from the Scratch library.

We will use a sound called **Dance Around**, which you can enter in the search bar or go to the **Loops** category. You can also use any other sound if you want: by clicking or hovering on the play buttons in the sound library, you can hear what they sound like!

### Step 4: Create a button

To make the card more of a surprise for the viewer, we will have a button that has to be clicked to open the card.

To make this button, select the paint icon from the sprite creator button.

Change the name of this sprite to something that suggests what it does, such as **button**. Change the **x** and **y** positions to both be 0.

You could use the button costume from the sprite library, but we will create our own using the rectangle tool.

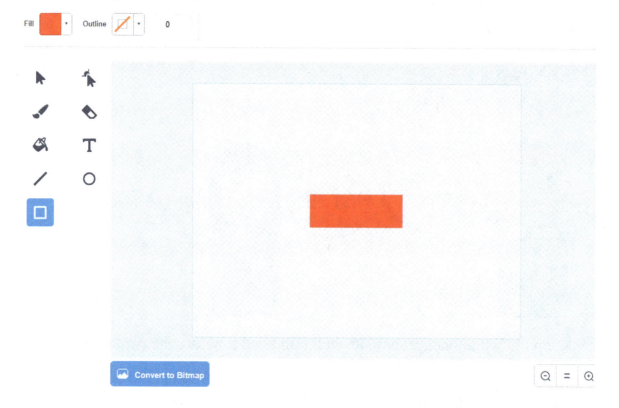

We also have a red button too, but you can use a different color. We will use the text tool to add a label. It can be something easy to understand such as 'open' or 'click me!'.

We have two scripts for the button – **when the green flag is clicked** and when the sprite itself is clicked.

When the green flag is clicked, we want to show the button and show a **say** block for about two seconds, with similar text to what is already in the button.

When the sprite is clicked, we want to hide it and switch to the party backdrop (as the starting backdrop will be white). After we've done those two things, we will **broadcast** a message called 'balloons', which our animated balloon sprites and backdrop will receive later on.

This is what the code will look like:

**Step 5: Changing the backdrop and playing sound**

When the green flag is clicked, we want to start with a plain white background for our button (this should be called **backdrop1**).

When the button is clicked, we will change to the party backdrop from that sprite.

When the balloons broadcast is received, we will play the **Dance Around** sound forever (unless the project is stopped).

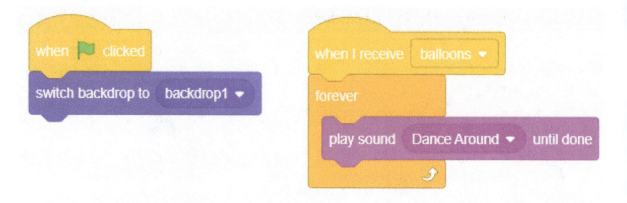

Now if you click the green flag, your button should look like this:

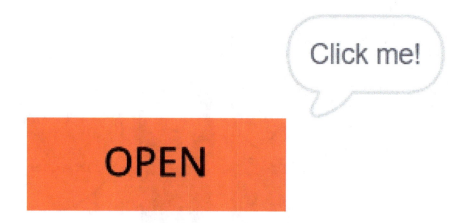

And when you click the sprite, the **Dance Around** sound should start playing and the backdrop should be the party room.

## Step 6: Adding text

When the card is opened, we want to show some text – for example, 'Happy Birthday'. We will also animate this sprite.

First of all, create a new sprite (by selecting the paint icon under the add button) and rename this sprite **text**. Change the **x** to 0 and the **y** to 70.

Under the **costumes** tab, we need to add the actual text. Use the text tool to write a message.

For our first script, we will hide the sprite, set the **x** and **y** positions and set the starting direction to point in (which is 90 degrees). This will be the done when the green flag is clicked.

The next script is for when the 'balloons' message is received. We will show the message (as the card will have now been opened) and we will continuously change the color of the sprite (using **the change color effect** block).

Finally, we will animate the text by changing the direction it's pointing in every few seconds.

These are the scripts we will use for the text sprite:

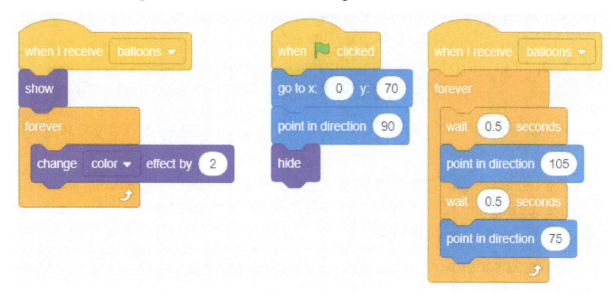

## Step 7: Animating balloons

The final step is to add animated balloons. In the Scratch sprite library, we have balloons which we will position next to the text and then send them upwards with a pop.

Go to the sprite library and search for the **balloon** sprite. This will be our first balloon.

Change the **x** to -192 and the **y** to -124.

When the green flag is clicked, we will hide the balloon sprite and move it to our starting **x** and **y** positions.

When the balloons message is received, we want to show the sprite, send it upwards using the **glide** block, **play** a pop sound when it reaches the top and then hide it again. While this is all happening, we will **change the color effect** at the same time.

This is the code for the first balloon:

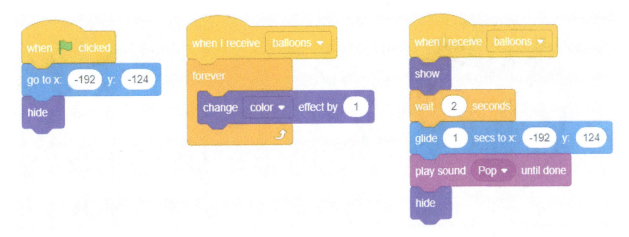

Take note that the **x** position stays the same but the **y** position doesn't have the minus, so it is just 124 instead of -124.

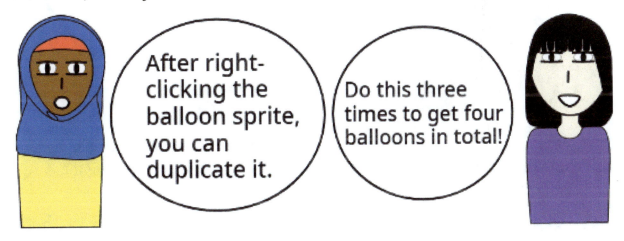

After right-clicking the balloon sprite, you can duplicate it.

Do this three times to get four balloons in total!

These are the coordinates for the second, third and fourth balloons:

Make sure the **x** coordinates are correct!

As well as the different coordinates, the amount of time for waiting before the balloons go up should be different by 1 second each – the first balloon waits two seconds, so the second will wait for three, the third for four and the fourth for five.

If you don't do a happy birthday card, you could do one for a special event, or to celebrate a success – it's up to you! Well done on completing the project!

**You can check your code in the section at the end of the book!**

# PROJECT 2 – FOOD CLICKER

Now for your next project – a food clicker! This is a simple project to create but will be fun to play later!

There is only one sprite – the item you need to click. It will have multiple costumes of different foods. The costume will change depending on how many clicks you've accumulated, and so will the background – it's like playing a game with multiple levels. At two certain checkpoints, you will also have autoclicks, to help level up faster.

If you'd like a headstart, follow the instructions depending on which editor you are using to download the start project.

## Online
1. Make sure you're signed into your Scratch account. Go to the following link: https://scratch.mit.edu/projects/926744782
2. Click the turquoise **Remix** button. You now have the basic sprites and backdrops for this project.

## Offline
1. Open your browser.
2. Go to the following link: https://scratch.mit.edu/projects/926744782/
3. Click the blue **See inside** button.
4. Click **File** and select Save to Your Computer. In the second step of the project, you will be able to load the starter material in the Scratch app.

## Step 1: Create a new project
To start this project, you will need to open Scratch. You can either sign into your Scratch account online or open the app on your device.

## Step 2: Load the starter project (offline only)
Once the Scratch editor is open, click **File** and select **Load from Your Computer**. Open the starter project from your file explorer.

## Step 3: Creating variables

Next, create two variables. **Clicks:**, for the number of times you've clicked on the sprite, and **cps**, for the number of autoclicks that will take place later on. Then set both variables to zero when the green flag is clicked:

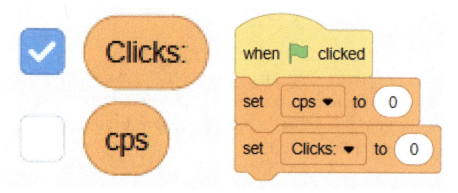

Remember to hide **cps** (by unchecking the box) and show **Clicks:**!

## Step 4: Making the backdrops

We will have six backdrops that we can change to. They can be different colors, or different designs. You can even use backdrops from the Scratch library!

These are the backdrops we're using!

Create about 6 of them, so that when you reach different amounts of clicks, the background changes.

Also, to reset everything when the project starts, add the script as shown below:

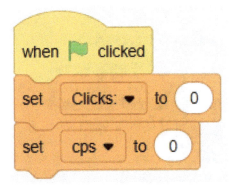

## Step 5: Creating the sprite

Paint a new sprite and call it something like **Food**. Go to the **Costumes** tab and add costumes from the sprite library. You can even create your own!

Add about 6 to 8, for some variety – but it can be more or less than that if you want!

Drag each costume to the cross to center it, and add the following script to ensure that:

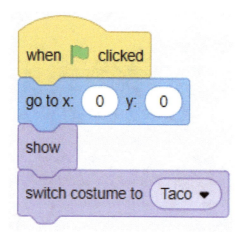

If you're not using the **Taco** costume, switch the costume to whichever one you're going to see first.

Let's add some action to the sprite. Under a **when this sprite clicked** block, add a **change variable by 1** block. It will be the variable where you store the number of clicks.

## Step 6: Levels based on clicks

Next, we want to change the costume depending on how many clicks you have – a sort of level system.

We will add the code to do this in a **forever** loop, using if conditions to check the number of clicks you've done. We'll do something similar for the backdrops too.

Here's an example of the code for the sprite you click and the backdrops, respectively:

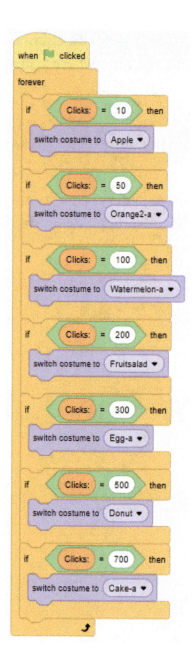

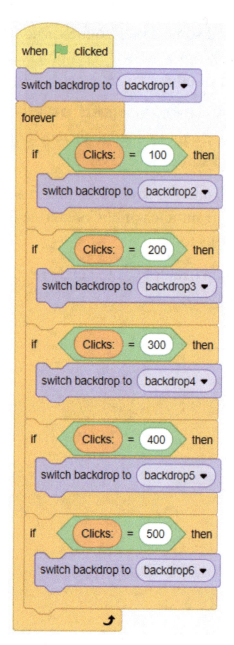

The first script checks the number of clicks in the variable and switches the costume according to the amount. The second script starts off with a default background, and as done for the main sprite to click, we change the backdrop as you 'level up'.

Add something similar to this in your project!

## Step 7: Autoclicks

This is the final step!

We need to start by adding the code to determine the number of autoclicks that are awarded to the player.

In a **forever** loop as we did with the 'levelling up' previously, we check the number of clicks already done.

We have only two conditions for auto-clicks - you can add more if you want!

Add the script below to your main sprite:

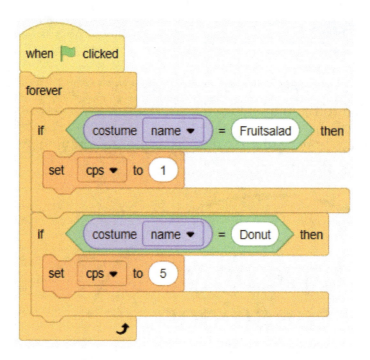

If you have different names for your costumes, make sure they match!

Just add this script to the backdrop to actually add the autoclicks to your current score:

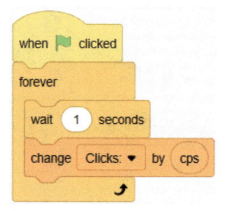

46

Well done on completing the project!

**You can check your code in the section at the end of the book!**

# PROJECT 3 – CRYSTAL COLLECTOR

Your third project is going to be a game – crystal collector! The aim of the game is to move the red triangle (the player) around the space, and when you touch a diamond, you can collect it! Moving side to side across the screen are three green circles which will try to hinder your progress and will end the game if you touch it!

This project will use some of the skills you used in the virtual card and the food clicker, such as **if** blocks and **variables**. You'll also be introduced to sensing blocks.

Below are the steps to download the starter project.

Follow the instructions for your editor below!

## Online

1. Make sure you're signed into your Scratch account. Go to the following link: https://scratch.mit.edu/projects/847444921/
2. Click the turquoise **Remix** button. You now have the basic sprites and backdrops for this project.

## Offline

1. Open your browser.
2. Go to the following link: https://scratch.mit.edu/projects/847444921/
3. Click the blue **See inside** button.
4. Click **File** and select Save to Your Computer. In the second step of the project, you will be able to load the starter material in the Scratch app.

## Step 1: Create a new project

To start this project, you will need to open Scratch. You can either sign into your Scratch account online or open the app on your device.

## Step 2: Load the starter project (offline only)

Once the Scratch editor is open, click **File** and select **Load from Your Computer**. Open the starter project from your file explorer.

## Step 3: Adding a backdrop

First of all, delete the cat sprite.

Next, add a background of your choice.

Delete the default white backdrop and create a new one with the paint button. Rename this new backdrop **Game Over**.

Create a black background using the rectangle tool and add white or red text saying the words 'Game Over'. It can look a bit like this:

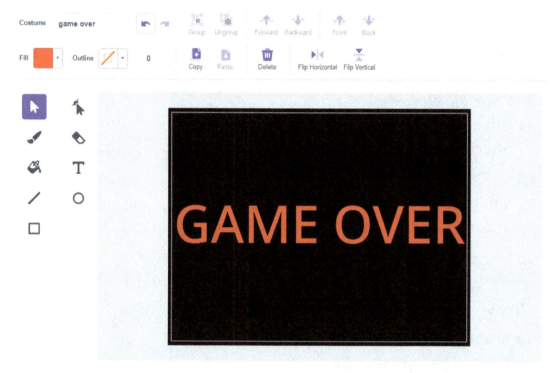

Under the **code** tab, add a **when green flag clicked** block, with a **switch backdrop** attached. When someone starts the game, we will automatically make sure the background is set to the one we imported from the library.

### Step 4: Creating the player sprite

Use the paint tool and create a new sprite. Call it **Player**.

Go to the **costumes** tab and select the rectangle tool. Change the fill to a color of your choice, and it's up to you whether or not you add an outline.

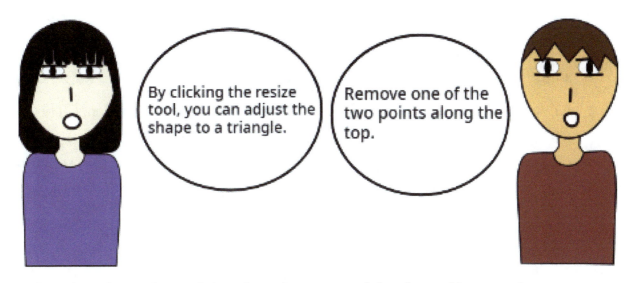

Speech bubble (left): By clicking the resize tool, you can adjust the shape to a triangle.

Speech bubble (right): Remove one of the two points along the top.

Select the other point and drag it to the center of the shape. You now have a triangle shape!

Create 3 copies of the shape. The second costume will be the triangle pointing to the right, costume3 will be to the left and the final costume will be pointing downwards (you can use the flip vertical tool for this).

Speech bubble: Time to add our first script! Yay!

Use a **when green flag clicked** block to show the sprite and move it to position of 238 along the **x** axis and 131 on the **y** axis. You may need to adjust this depending on the size of your player.

After the **go to** block, we need a **forever** loop with four **if** statements. This is where the use of **conditionals** and **sensors** comes into play.

Under the **sensing** tab, find the block that says, **key space pressed?**. We will change the space (from the dropdown list) to right, left, up and down arrow keys. Switch costumes accordingly to the directions.

Your code will look similar to this:

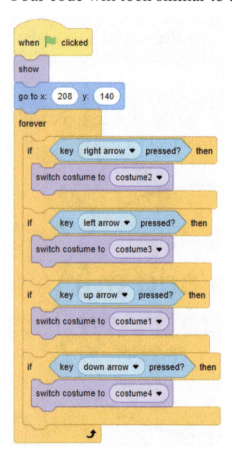

To actually make the sprite move, we can use the **change x** and **change y** blocks. This will update the coordinates of the player, and by doing this in a

**forever** block, these four conditions are repeatedly checked over and over until all scripts in the project are stopped.

For the right arrow, the **x** changes by 10, the left arrow by -10, and the same for the up and down arrow keys, but it's the **y** axis instead of the **x** axis.

### Step 5: Adding crystals and a variable

We need to create a variable to keep score. Go to the **variables** tab on the left and make a new variable. Call it **crystals** (or right-click the **my variable** variable and rename it, then click the checkmark to show it).

From the stage, right-click the crystals variable and change to a 'large readout'.

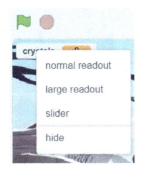 A large readout looks like this:

For the actual crystals, add a new sprite from the sprite library. Search 'crystal' to find it. We want to use the two costumes but for different things. The blue crystal will be what we are collecting, and the purple crystal will be for the variable.

Paint a new sprite and you can call it whatever you want (this will be for the crystal that shows how many we have, alongside the variable).

53

From the first **Crystal** sprite, go to the purple crystal and drag it across to the sprite you just created. This will duplicate the costume in the other sprite, and so now you can remove it from the original **Crystal**, and **costume1** from **Crystal2**.

Adjust the positioning of the purple crystal so it comes up alongside the large readout of the **crystals** variable.

Once you've got it into place, add the following code:

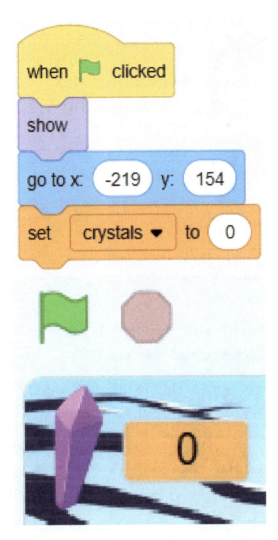

This will make sure the crystal is shown, the variable is set to zero when the game is started, and the position is what you've moved it to be. Alongside the code is also how the crystal could be positioned.

Back in the blue crystal sprite, we will just add a **when green flag clicked** block, show, and tell it to go to a random position, like so:

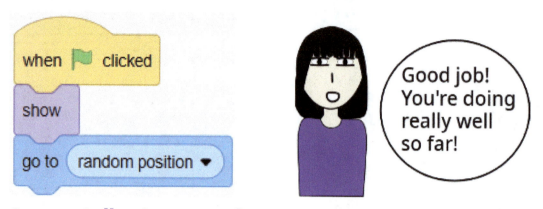

## Step 6: Collecting crystals

Now that we've got a variable to keep score, a moving player, and a crystal to collect, we want to actually earn some points as we control our player to get those crystals!

We will use a **forever** block to continuously check if our player is touching a crystal, and to award points, broadcast a message and play a sound.

First of all, go to the **sounds** tab of the **Player** sprite. Delete the **pop** sound and add a new sound from the Scratch library. You can find **collect** by searching for it or going to the **Effects** tab.

Return to the code tab and add a **when green flag clicked** block. Add a **forever** block, and inside, an **if** conditional.

Go to the **sensing** tab (like we did earlier with the arrow keys blocks) and add the block which says **touching mouse-pointer?**. Put it in the space that the **if ... then** block gives. From the dropdown menu, change the mouse-pointer to the **Crystal** sprite.

Like we said previously in this step, we need a **change crystals by 1** block from the **variables** tab, a **broadcast** block, and a **play sound** block. Add all three into the conditional, in that order.

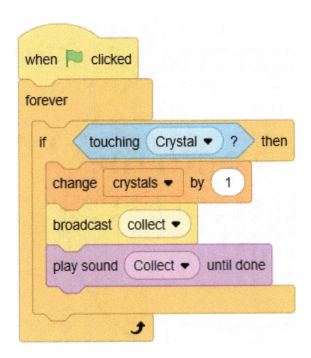

Go to the **Crystal** sprite. We want to move the position of the crystal after it's been collected, so that we can travel across the stage to collect more points.

Use the **when I receive** block and another **go to random position** block to do this.

## Step 7: Adding an obstacle

Paint a new sprite. You don't need to name it, but you can if you wish to do so.

Go to the costumes tab if you're not on it already and create a coloured circle. It can be however big you want it to be.

Next, go to the **sounds** tab and from the Scratch sound library, you can add the **Zoop** sound, by searching for it or going to the **Effects** tab. Make sure to delete the **pop** sound first, as we won't be using it in the project.

Return to the code tab, so that we can start adding some scripts!

First of all, we need to make the circle move, and set it to a default position. The following code does the trick:

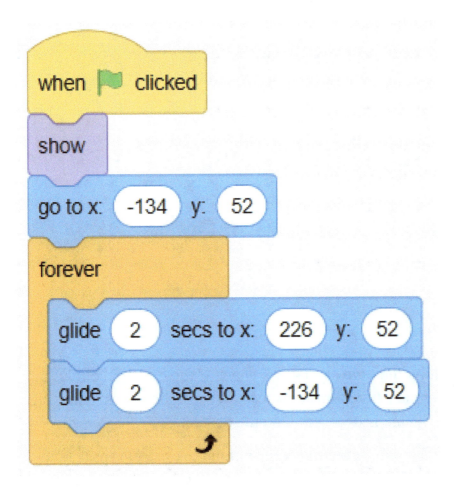

We show the obstacle, set it to a default position, and continuously make it glide back and forth across the screen. Where it shows up all depends on the size, and how you've positioned the circle in the **costumes** tab. It's best to place it in the center (where the cross is; the Scratch editor can automatically shift your shape into place when you drag it in that direction!).

To end the game when it's touched, we can do a similar thing as we did with detecting whether the player has come into contact with the **Crystal** or not – a forever and an **if … then** condition.

This is the code:

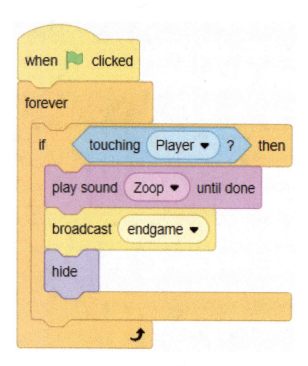

So, instead of touching the blue crystal, we check if the coloured circle (the obstacle) is touching the **Player** sprite instead. We also broadcast a message to all sprites that the game is over and hide the obstacle.

We want to receive that **endgame** message within the obstacle sprite, and then hide it. Add the correct code for that. Add this code to the blue crystal sprite and the **Player** sprite as well.

However, for the **Player** sprite, also add this block:

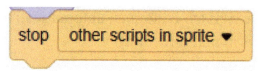

This will stop all the other scripts in the **Player** sprite from running.

## Step 8: Adding other obstacles and showing the game over screen

We will duplicate the coloured circle twice. Adjust the **y** axes like so:

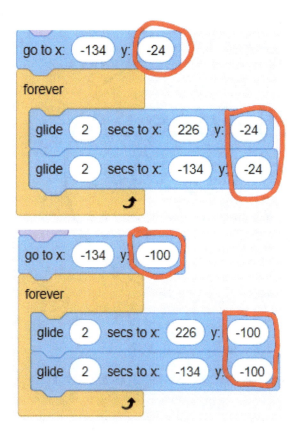

If you go to the code tab of the backdrop, add this script:

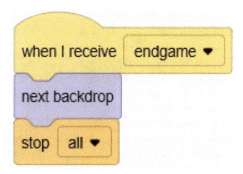

This will ensure that absolutely everything in the game has been stopped to show the game over screen!

Congratulations on coming this far!

**You can check your code in the section at the end of the book!**

# PROJECT 4 – FOOD FIGHT!

Welcome to the second to last project – another game with a theme of food! The aim of the game is to move your player past moving obstacles to reach the checkpoint. The obstacles are, as you've probably guessed, items of food. It's a pretty simple project and will be fun to play afterwards!

In this project, we mainly use sensing blocks to detect where your player is, and also use motion blocks for the obstacles.

If you'd like to get ahead and start coding right away, you can follow the instructions below to download the starter project for your environment.

## Online

1. Make sure you're signed into your Scratch account. Go to the following link: https://scratch.mit.edu/projects/941652495/
2. Click the turquoise **Remix** button. You now have the basic sprites and backdrops for this project.

## Offline

1. Open your browser.
2. Go to the following link: https://scratch.mit.edu/projects/941652495/
3. Click the blue **See inside** button.
4. Click **File** and select Save to Your Computer. In the second step of the project, you will be able to load the starter material in the Scratch app.

## Step 1: Create a new project

To start this project, you will need to open Scratch. You can either sign into your Scratch account online or open the app on your device.

## Step 2: Load the starter project (offline only)

Once the Scratch editor is open, click **File** and select **Load from Your Computer**. Open the starter project from your file explorer.

## Step 3: Creating backdrops

Start off by deleting the cat sprite.

We're going to have four backdrops – a welcome screen, a basic background during the game and a win or loss backdrop, depending on the player's result.

Name the backdrops however you want!

We use a circle and the reshape tool to create the '1' we show – you don't need to include it if you don't want to!

The code for the backdrop is really simple – we receive a few messages, change some backdrops and one script to end the project.

Add these blocks:

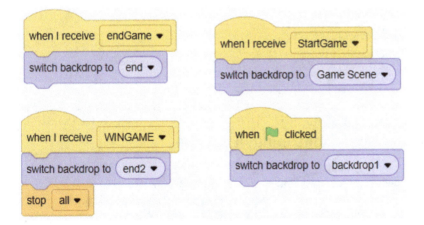

## Step 4: Creating a play button

Paint a new sprite and name it **play**. Think of your typical play button – a triangle in a circle. This is the sort of design we want to go for.

The scripts will be fairly simple. We set a starting position and add a **when this sprite clicked** to send the **StartGame** broadcast to the backdrop.

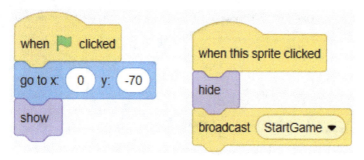

## Step 5: Creating the player

Now we want to create our player. Similar to what we did in the Crystal Collector project, we'll just have a green circle, rather than a red triangle. It will be controlled by the arrow keys.

Start with these scripts:

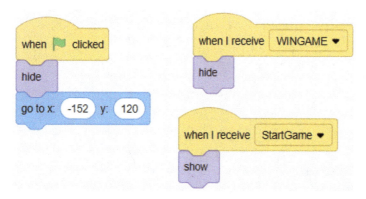

This will show and hide the player as appropriate and set it's default position too. You can also name the sprite something like **player**.

I called mine 'You'!

## Step 6: Adding a checkpoint

For the checkpoint, we'll have another coloured circle. Paint the sprite as appropriate.

These scripts show and hide the checkpoint at the right times and set its starting position:

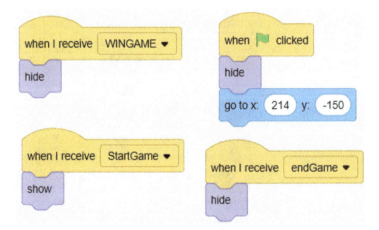

## Step 7: Making obstacles

We will have six obstacles. In the starter project, there are two of each: **Spinning Banana**, **Swinging Apple,** and **Slicing Bread**. We use the **turn** block for the bananas and the bread, and **glide** blocks for the apples.

These sprites can be found in the Scratch costume library. You can use whichever foods you want, it doesn't have to be the ones mentioned here!

Here's what we do for each sprite:

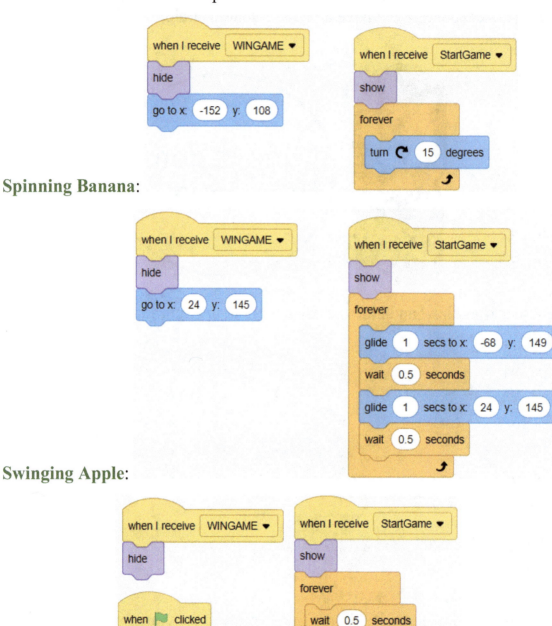

**Spinning Banana**:

**Swinging Apple**:

**Slicing Bread**:

## Step 8: Coding the player

Now that we have our obstacles, backdrops, and a checkpoint we need to reach, we now need to be able to control the player and detect whether it's touching an obstacle or the checkpoint.

You can add these blocks to the **checkpoint** sprite:

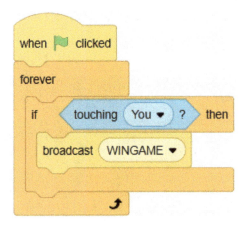

Through the conditional, this checks whether or not the checkpoint has been touched by the player sprite yet, done through the **sensing** block we use as the condition. If that's **true**, we broadcast the **WINGAME** message, which you would've already seen in previous steps.

Now we need to add the code to actually reach that checkpoint and win the game.

Upon receiving the message that the game has started, we use a **forever** loop to continuously detect when an arrow key is pressed. The **sensing** section has a block that will do exactly what we want. To move the player, we just change the **x** and **y** values using **motion** blocks.

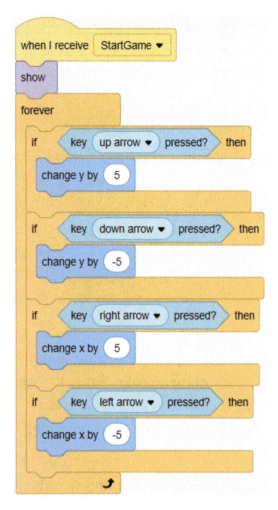

Don't forget to check which **change …** block you've added to the script!

Again, under a **when I receive StartGame** block, and within a **forever** loop, we use conditions again to make some decisions. The decision we make on this script is to end the game if you touch an obstacle.

Here's an example:

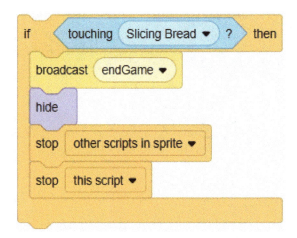

As well as doing this for the **Slicing Bread**, repeat it for the other two obstacles as well.

## Step 9: More obstacles

To add more obstacles, simply duplicate the banana, apple, and bread. You can do this however many times you like. You could also just add new foods as obstacles.

We just have two of each obstacle.

In the **You** sprite, you just need to duplicate the previous conditions you used and change the name of the sprite from the dropdown.

Congratulations, you've finished another project!

**You can check your code in the section at the end of the book!**

# PROJECT 5 – QUIZ

The final project is a quiz! The goal for this project is simple – display some questions and select the correct answers. At the end of the project, you show the score out of 6 (or however many questions you choose to have).

You will reuse skills from the other projects in this book – conditionals make a notable appearance in this project!

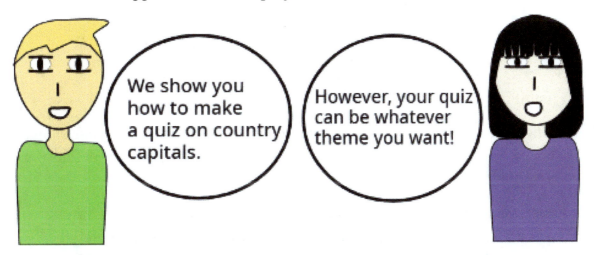

This project will be a little complicated, so it might be a good idea to go through all the steps first before making your quiz! Take notes and plan beforehand!

Follow the instructions to download the starter project for your chosen environment below!

## Online

1. Make sure you're signed into your Scratch account. Go to the following link: https://scratch.mit.edu/projects/922923401/
2. Click the turquoise **Remix** button. You now have the basic sprites and backdrops for this project.

## Offline

1. Open your browser.
2. Go to the following link: https://scratch.mit.edu/projects/922923401/

3. Click the blue **See inside** button.
4. Click **File** and select Save to Your Computer. In the second step of the project, you will be able to load the starter material in the Scratch app.

## Step 1: Create a new project

To start this project, you will need to open Scratch. You can either sign into your Scratch account online or open the app on your device.

## Step 2: Load the starter project (offline only)

Once the Scratch editor is open, click **File** and select **Load from Your Computer**. Open the starter project from your file explorer.

## Step 3: Creating backdrops

First of all, delete the cat sprite.

Using the rectangle tool, fill the backdrop space with a color of your choice. Change the name of the backdrop to **question**. This will be your default background.

Duplicate it and change the background color to green and add 'Correct Answer' text. Copy and paste this new backdrop, this time changing the color to red and changing 'correct' to 'incorrect'. Rename the backdrops accordingly.

Now we will create the relevant score backdrops.

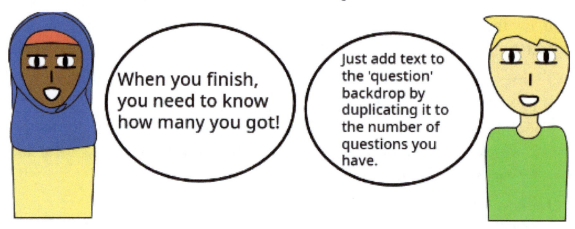

When you finish, you need to know how many you got!

Just add text to the 'question' backdrop by duplicating it to the number of questions you have.

In this project, we create six questions. However, you have the freedom to have as many as you want!

Add text, for instance: 'your score: 6' or similar. Name the backdrops from 0 to the number of questions you'll have. Make sure to change the number of the score!

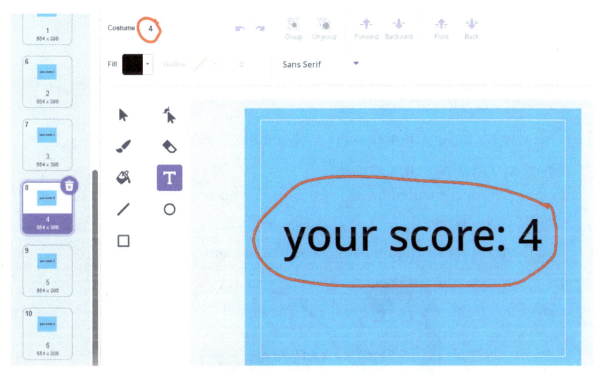

## Step 4: Creating variables

Create these two variables: **qnumber** (for the number of the current question) and **score** (to know which backdrop to display at the end).

Make sure both variables are hidden (uncheck the boxes).

Now that we've created the variables, add this script to the backdrop:

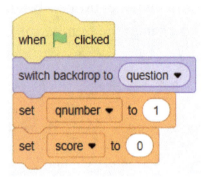

This will set the question number to 1 and the score to 0!

## Step 5: Adding questions

Paint a new sprite called **questions**. This is where we will add the relevant text for each question.

Use the text tool and add however many questions you want.

Make sure to center the text by dragging it to the cross.

Let's add some code.

**When the green flag is clicked**, we want to show the **questions** sprite, switch to the first question and position the questions.

Use the following script:

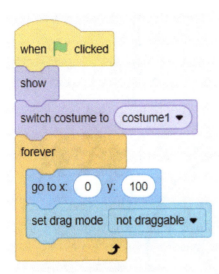

## Step 6: Creating answer buttons

Paint another new sprite. We will have one costume for each question. Create rectangles and add text inside them for your different answers. The first costume will correlate with the first question, the second costume to the second question, and so on. Use different colors (or shapes and fonts) too!

Once we've added some relevant code, we will duplicate this sprite twice for the other options.

Here's an example of how the buttons might look (alongside a question):

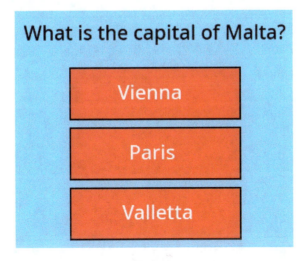

Make sure you know which of the three buttons will have the correct answer for every question!

The scripts we will add will be very similar to what we did for the questions sprite (**when green flag clicked**).

We'll also add scripts for when the sprite is clicked, and a few for when certain messages are received (later on).

Name the sprites something like **answers1**. Don't forget to center the costumes to the cross!

Create all six costumes for the first button.

Here's one way to do it:

The possible answers to all six questions are added as buttons in the single sprite. We will use the code (later on!) to determine which of these is the correct option for each question.

This will be our **when green flag clicked** script:

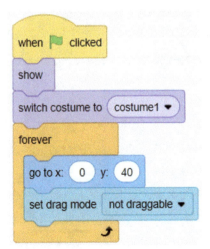

79

## Step 7: Broadcasts

Let's get started with creating our broadcast messages.

When you click on the answer button, you need to know if your answer is correct. We can use broadcasts to tell other sprites to hide, and the relevant backdrop to show.

The broadcasts we'll be using will include one for correct and incorrect answers, another as a prompt to move on to the next question and two for the final incorrect and correct answers.

Add these scripts to your button sprite and questions sprite:

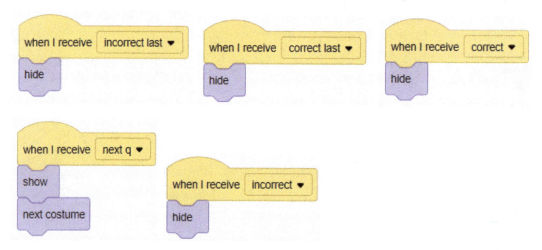

The scripts we will add for the backdrop is as explained before: changing to either correct or incorrect, as well as changing your score and the question number. At the end of that, we add a broadcast to change to the next question.

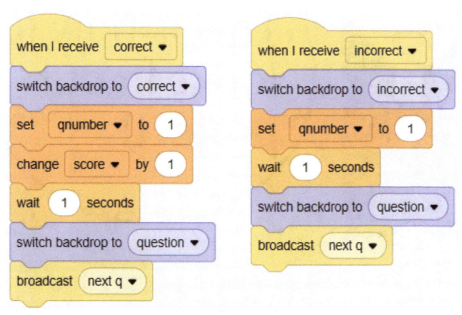

## Step 8: 'when this sprite clicked'

To actually broadcast these messages, we need to detect when the button has been clicked on. To do this we can use **when this sprite clicked** block to check. Following this, we will make use of nested conditionals. We check what number question we're on and decide whether or not the current button is the correct answer for that question. In the last **if-else**, you broadcast the correct or incorrect message that has **last** following it.

This is how it looks in our project!

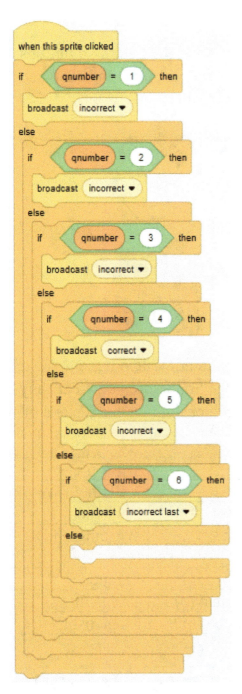

It seems a little confusing at first, but to make it easier for yourself, you can write down your questions and answers first. For each question, include three possible answers. More on this in the coming steps!

## Step 9: **Adding other buttons**

We've coded the first button, so now you need to add the other two buttons to the project. You can simply duplicate the first button sprite and change the text, colors, broadcasts, and positions as applicable.

We use a y of -20 for the second button and y -80 for the third.

In the previous step, it was mentioned that you should write out the questions and answers before you add the scripts. So, before you create any more buttons and write the script mentioned previously, you can make a plan that looks something like this:

| Questions | Option A | Option B | Option C |
|---|---|---|---|
| Malta | Vienna | Paris | Valletta (c) |
| Morocco | Casablanca | Rabat (c) | Baghdad |
| America | New York | Tehran | Washington DC (c) |
| Montenegro | Podgorica (c) | Tirana | Prague |
| Kazakhstan | Bishkek | Nur-Sultan (c) | Tashkent |
| Tajikistan | Ashgabat | Dushanbe (c) | Mogadishu |

The **c** represents correct. Don't forget to ensure there is a correct answer for all the options for each question!

## Step 10: Displaying the final score

This is the final step, and it's showing the player how many points they've accumulated in the quiz. Essentially, we will have two broadcasts that receive the messages **incorrect last** or **correct last**. For a final correct answer, it will award the point as it should and display the **correct** backdrop. For a final incorrect answer, it will just show the **incorrect** backdrop. After showing whether or not you got the question right or wrong, it then shows your score, between 0 and 6.

These are the scripts:

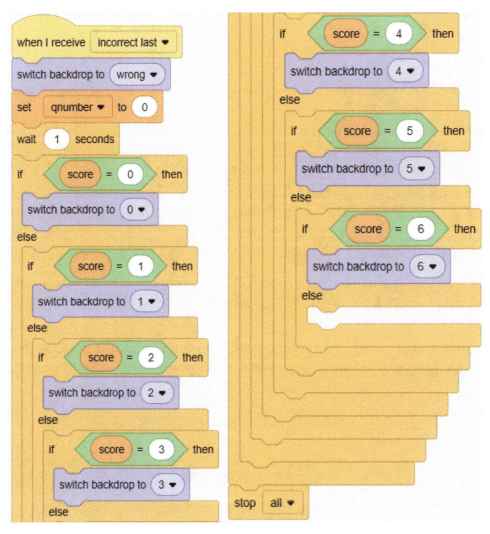

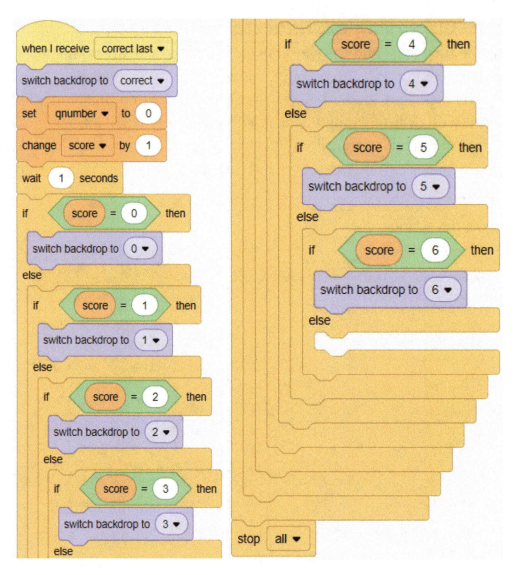

Go through the steps in this project again to make sure you understand and have everything together!

Good job finishing this project!

**You can check your code in the section at the end of the book!**

# COMPLETE CODE

In this chapter, all sprites, backdrops and scripts used for the projects in this book are shown here for reference! Project demo links are also available at the end!

## Project 1: Virtual Card

Sprites and backdrops

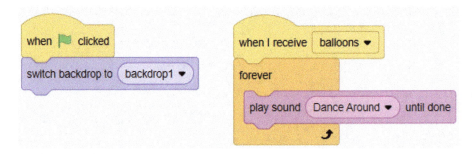

Backdrop scripts

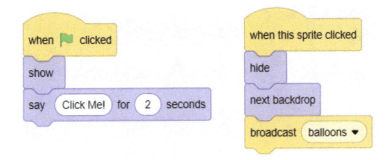

'Click Me' scripts

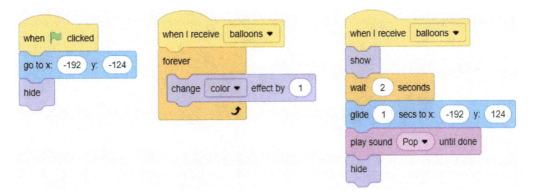

Balloon scripts

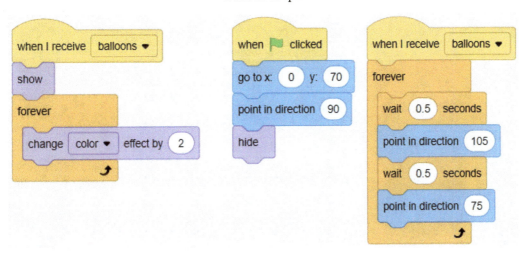

'Happy birthday' sprite scripts

# Project 2: Food Clicker

Sprite and backdrops

'Food sprite' costumes

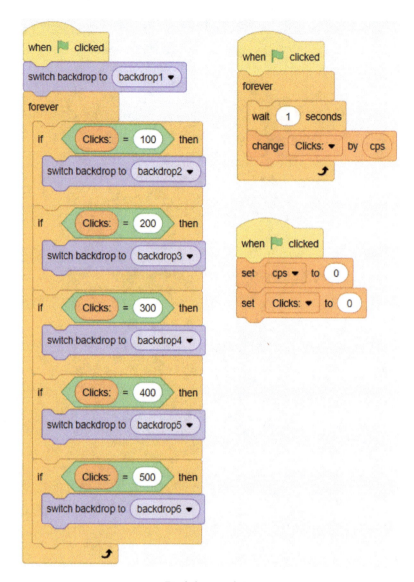

Backdrop scripts

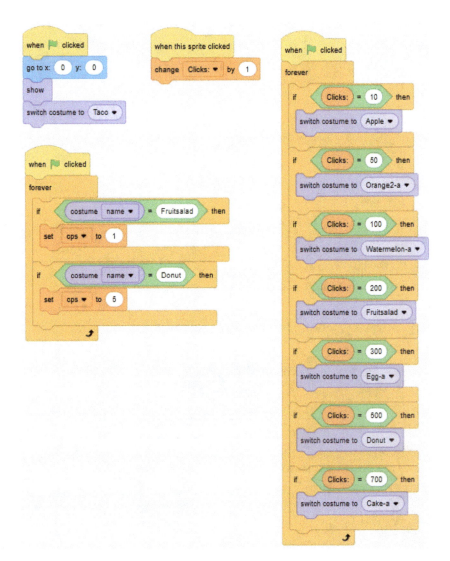

'Food' sprite scripts

# Project 3: Crystal Collector

Sprites and backdrops

'Player' sprite costumes

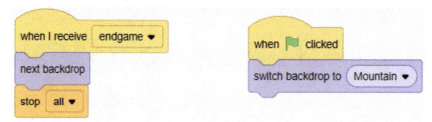

Backdrop scripts

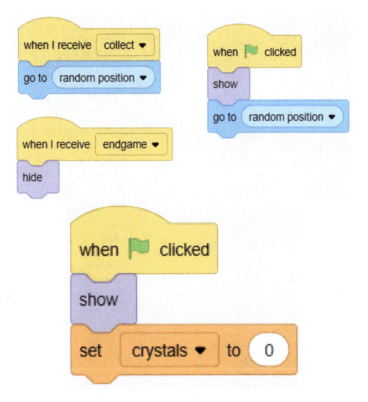

Scripts for 'Crystal' and 'Crystal2', respectively

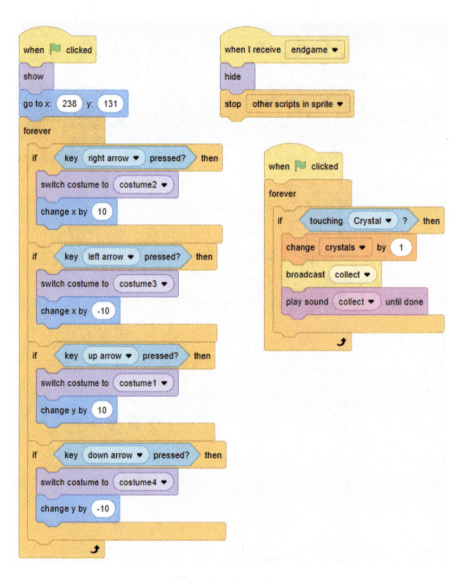

'Player' sprites scripts

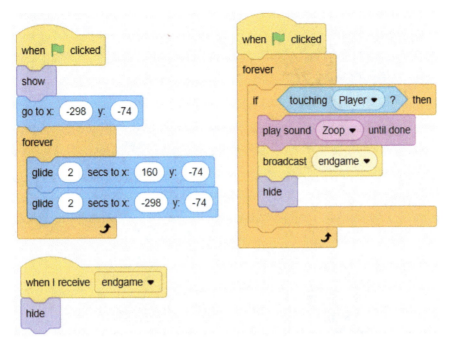

Obstacle scripts

# Project 4: **Food Fight!**

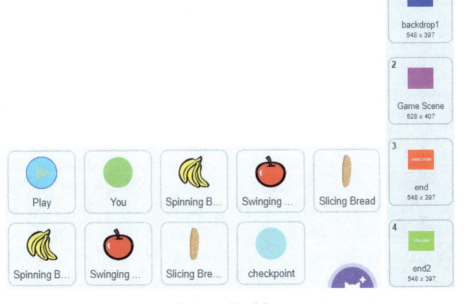

Sprites and backdrops

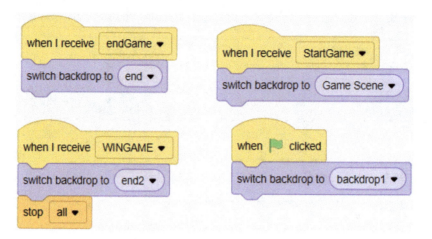

Backdrop scripts

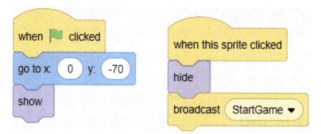

'Play' sprite scripts

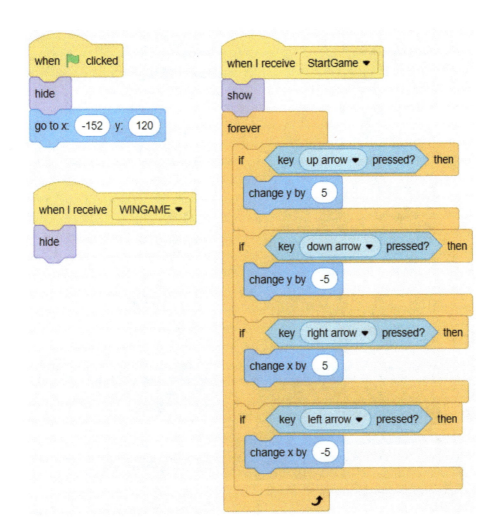

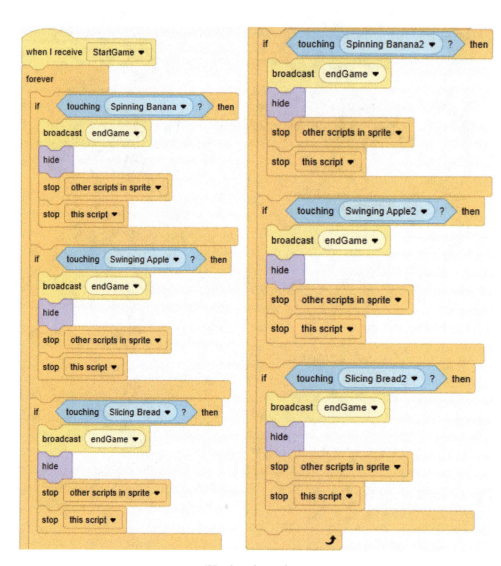

'You' sprite scripts

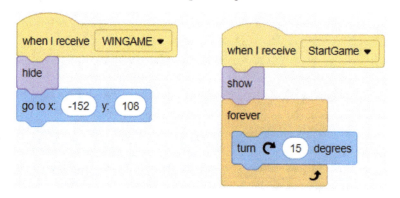

'Spinning Banana' scripts

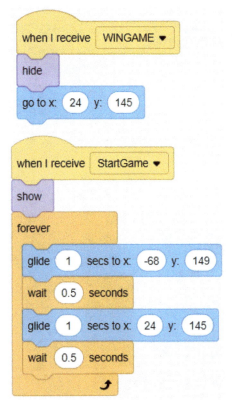

'Swinging Apple' scripts

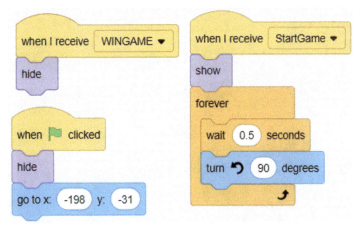

'Slicing Bread' scripts

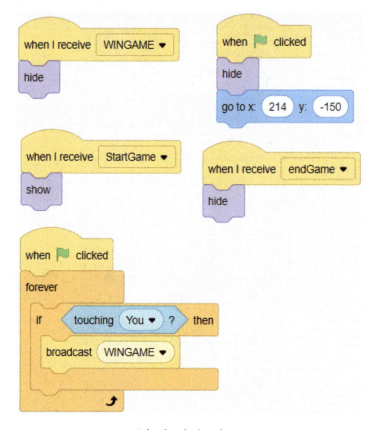

'checkpoint' scripts

## Project 5: Quiz

questions   answers1   answers2   answers3

Sprites

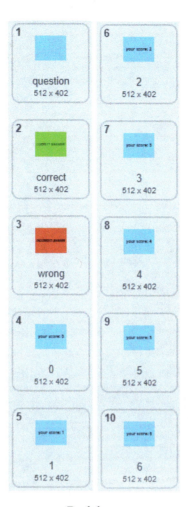

Backdrops

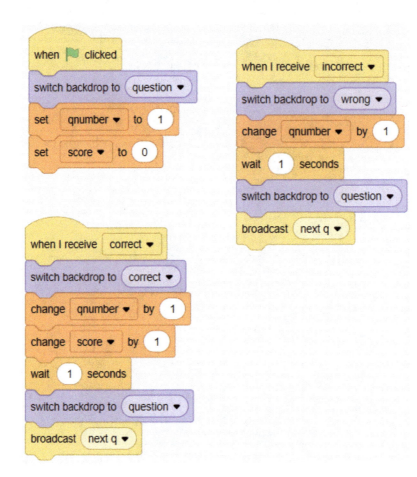

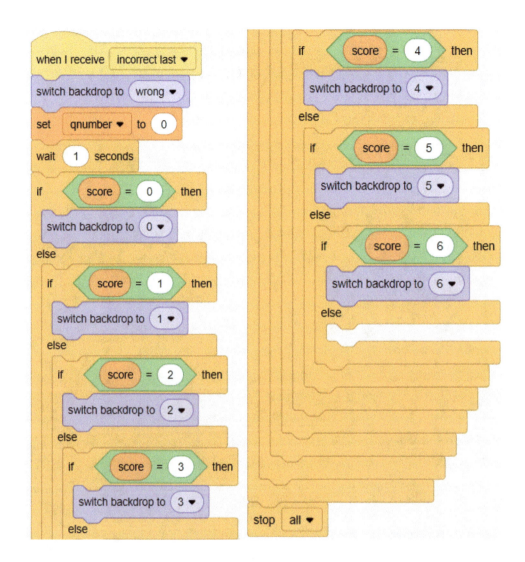

when I receive [incorrect last ▼]

switch backdrop to [wrong ▼]

set [qnumber ▼] to (0)

wait (1) seconds

if < (score) = (0) > then
  switch backdrop to (0 ▼)
else
  if < (score) = (1) > then
    switch backdrop to (1 ▼)
  else
    if < (score) = (2) > then
      switch backdrop to (2 ▼)
    else
      if < (score) = (3) > then
        switch backdrop to (3 ▼)
      else
        if < (score) = (4) > then
          switch backdrop to (4 ▼)
        else
          if < (score) = (5) > then
            switch backdrop to (5 ▼)
          else
            if < (score) = (6) > then
              switch backdrop to (6 ▼)
            else

stop [all ▼]

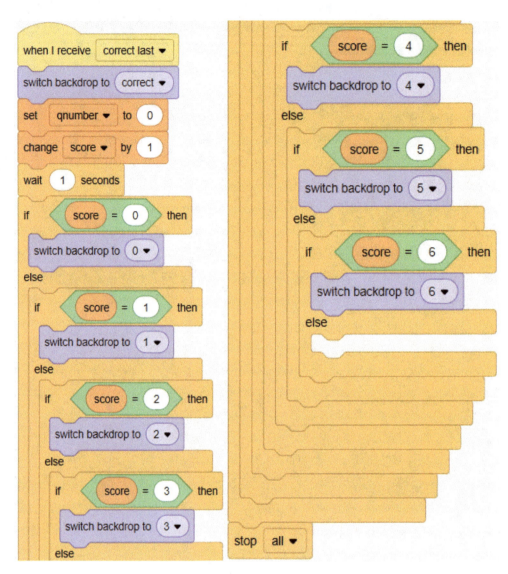

Backdrop scripts

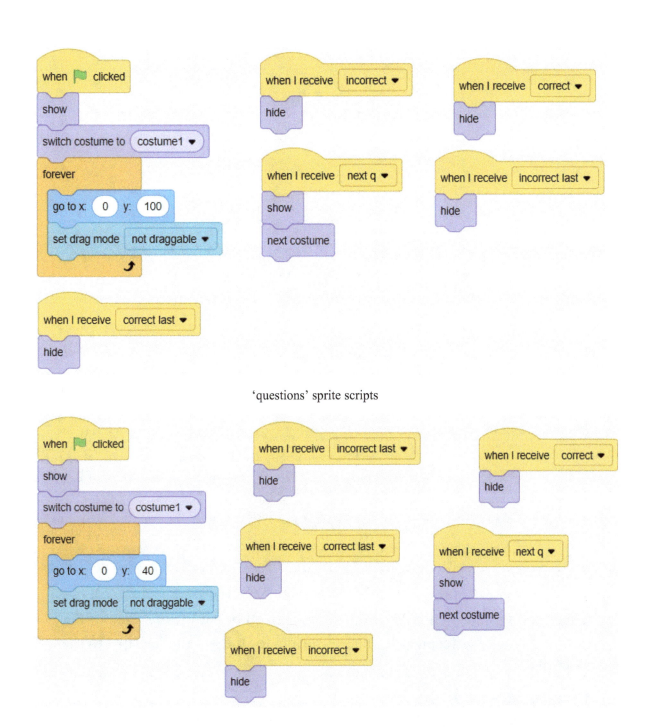

'questions' sprite scripts

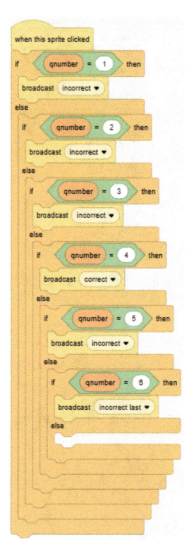

Example of answer button scripts

Check the Project 5 chapter or the demo (linked below) for an idea of the design of each sprite, and alternative scripts for the buttons' scripts to the example.

## Project demo links

Project 1 (Virtual Card): https://scratch.mit.edu/projects/843824640/

Project 2 (Food Clicker): https://scratch.mit.edu/projects/925911345/

Project 3 (Crystal Collector): https://scratch.mit.edu/projects/844486190/

Project 4 (Food Fight!): https://scratch.mit.edu/projects/928294118/

Project 5 (Quiz): https://scratch.mit.edu/projects/920071258/

# BONUS CHAPTER: TIPS, TRICKS AND MORE!

To help you go further in your Scratch journey, we've compiled this chapter with tweaks you can make to the project, and other tips and tricks you can use when you're coding with Scratch!

## Virtual Card

In the virtual card project, you could change the text and colors for different occasions or celebrations. Here's an example:

You could also change the music to whatever you like.

By changing the color effect to 10 (in the text or balloon) sprites, you get a faster animation. **Strobe light warning.**

## Food Clicker

By adding more costumes or backdrops, you can add more levels and autoclickers.

Another thing you could try is to make the sprite you click on get bigger for a moment, before returning to normal size. You can change the **when this sprite clicked** script to something like this:

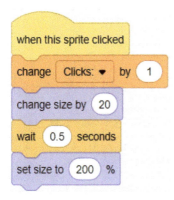

## Crystal Collector

You can duplicate the green circles for more obstacles or find other costumes from the Scratch library. You can even make your own!

You could add the purple crystal as another collectible, or possibly a potion, that gives bonus points.

Instead of instantly ending the game when you touch an obstacle (especially if you increase the number of them), you could incorporate a lives system. Here's how:

1. Create a **lives** variable.

2. Add this to the **player** sprite:

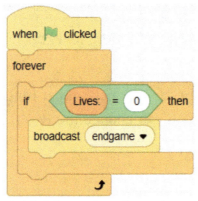

3. Add this to the obstacle sprites:

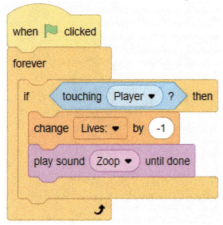

4. Change your **when green flag clicked** in the backdrop's code to this:

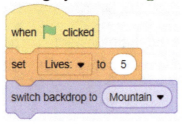

5. Test the game!

## Food Fight

Below is an example of a script for an additional obstacle, **Inflating Orange**:

1. Add the orange sprite (or create your own!).
2. Use similar scripts as done with other obstacles:

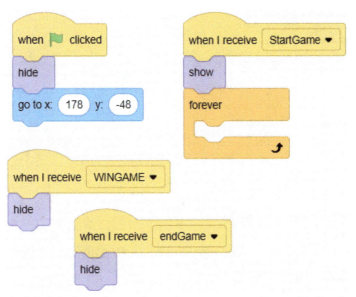

3. Add this block to the **when green flag clicked** script:

4. Write this script in the empty **forever** loop:

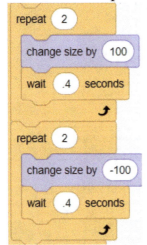

This will gradually increase the size of the orange, and then decrease it.

5. Add this conditional to the **You** sprite:

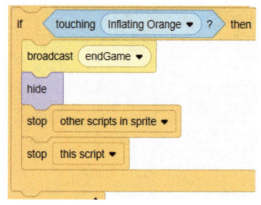

6. Try playing with the new obstacle!

After you reach the first checkpoint, you can move onto another level. Look at the steps below to add another level:

1. Create a new backdrop and make it different from the first level.
2. Instead of broadcasting **WINGAME** if the checkpoint touches the **You** sprite, changing it to a **NEXTLEVEL** broadcast:

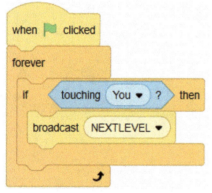

3. Change the backdrop when that broadcast is received:

4. Add this script to **You** to return the player to the starting position:

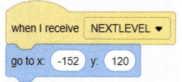

5. If you want, you can change the action of obstacles in another level. Here's an example with a **Spinning Banana**:

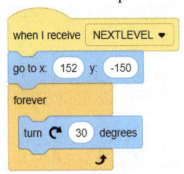

6. Try out your game with the new level!

You can also add music – the Scratch audio library has some good beats! As you level up, you can change backdrops as well.

## Quiz

In this project, you can add additional questions and change designs. You could have more options. Don't forget to plan beforehand!

## Other tips and tricks

Always think about the order you're placing your code in Scratch – it only runs code in the order you put it in! This is why in some projects we use **when green flag clicked** more than once for one sprite to run the scripts at the same time.

Drag elements of a costume to the cross in the editor to center them.

Use a **go to** block in a **forever** loop so a sprite never moves.

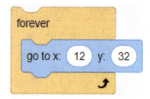

Using a **start sound …** block allows you to continue with the code while a sound is playing. **play sound …** will play the entire audio until it's finished before continuing with your script.

Using a **forever** and **change color** block with a value of 1 can make a smooth, satisfying effect.

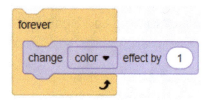

**Sensing** blocks are really helpful when paired with a conditional.

By placing a **go to front layer** block in a **forever**, other sprite will never go on top of a specific sprite.

The **answer** block from the **sensing** category can help you store responses from the **ask** block in variables. This is an example of a script you can use:

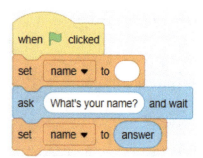

The **clear graphic effects** block resets any changes made by **change …
effect** and **set … effect**.

Instead of multiple conditionals with the same actions in the **if** or **else**
sections, you can use **and** and **or** blocks (from the **operators** section). This
is how it would look with the obstacle conditionals in the Food Fight project:

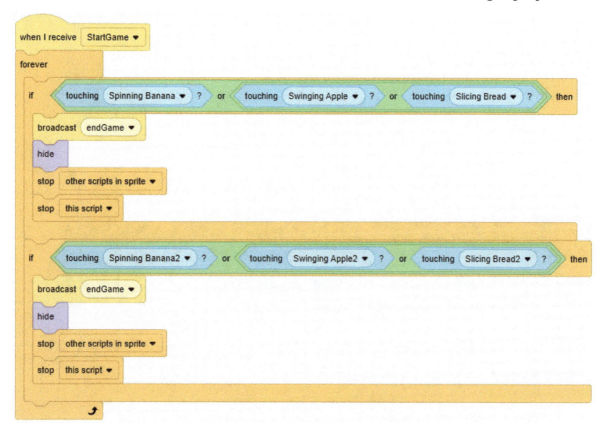

To add more **and**s or **or**s, you can simply nest them, as done in the example
above.

The **length of …** and **letter # of …** blocks (from **operators**) can help you
see how long a variable is (as a **string**) or find which position a certain
number or letter is in a value.

By pairing a **mouse down?** block with a condition, you can check whether
or not the someone left-clicks on their mouse.

Explore **operators** and **sensing** – there's so many blocks that can be used for many things!

# WHAT NEXT?

Throughout this book, you've learnt to make games and animations using Scratch. Well done and congratulations, you've tried really hard!

We hope this has shown you how exciting and wonderful coding is, and the great things that you can create – this book is only just the beginning! You've gained various skills in each section, and we hope this will encourage you to make even more fantastic things in the (not too far) future.

If you want to continue your coding journey, there are many excellent resources on the Internet which are available to you. Here are just a few:

- https://w3schools.com – if you would like to get into other programming languages asides Scratch!
- https://justcodaborate.org – visit our website to get involved in bootcamps and workshops!
- https://scratch.mit.edu and the Scratch Team YouTube channel – you can learn more about creating in Scratch!
- Coding with Rumaysa on YouTube – if you would like to learn some more Scratch and beyond!

**Thank you for reading and learning from this book, we hope you enjoyed it!**

# ABOUT THE AUTHORS

## Rumaysa Ahmed

**Rumaysa Ahmed** is a children's author and illustrator. *Starting From Scratch* is her fifth book.

Her first book is *Complete Web Applications using PHP and MySQL*, which was published in December 2019, and her second is *Build an E-commerce Website*, which was published in April 2020. Rumaysa's third book was *Coding for Kids*, published December 2020. Her first illustrated work was *Muhammad and Michael's Mischievous Mind*, and her debut novel was *Rachel Inside Out*, published 2021 and 2022, respectively.

Rumaysa is the founder of JUSTCodaborate, a not-for-profit organization aiming to provide education for children and teenagers in ICT, computer programming, science, and engineering.

You can find out more on her website, https://www.rumaysaahmed.com.

## Zayd Ahmed

**Zayd Ahmed** is a children's author. *Muhammad and Michael's Mischievous Mind* is his first book and debut novel. *Starting From Scratch* is his second book. Zayd is also a co-founder of JUSTCodaborate, a not-for-profit organisation aiming to provide education for children and teenagers in ICT, computer programming, science, and engineering.

www.ingramcontent.com/pod-product-compliance
Lightning Source LLC
La Vergne TN
LVHW081346050326
832903LV00024B/1350